LISTENING TO THE STARS
Jocelyn Bell Burnell
Discovers Pulsars

Jodie Parachini

ILLUSTRATED BY Alexandra Badiu

ALBERT WHITMAN & COMPANY
CHICAGO, ILLINOIS

Does the galaxy have a sound?

Is it loud and full of thunderous booms?
Soft murmurings, whooshing whispers?
Blips and bloops, like laughter and hiccups?

Silent?

When Jocelyn Bell was young,
she never dreamed that she would spend
her life listening to the stars.

But sometimes, if you open your mind,
you can hear the universe.

Jocelyn Bell was born in 1943 in Northern Ireland. She lived on a farm in a house nicknamed Solitude, but there was rarely any solitude on that happy farm—Jocelyn had a sister, two brothers, a dog, and many cats.

As a young child, Jocelyn loved to read. Her father brought home many different kinds of books from the library, but the ones Jocelyn liked most were about astronomy. She read everything she could find about stars and galaxies, planets and space.

The teachers at Jocelyn's school didn't think girls should study science. They thought cooking and sewing were more appropriate subjects for girls. "Physics is far too complicated," they said. "You won't understand it."

On the first day, Jocelyn and two of her friends stood up. "We want to switch to the boys' class," they announced.

Surprisingly, the principal of the school agreed, and by the time she was twelve, Jocelyn was the best student in the class. This was the first time Jocelyn stood up for something she wanted, but it wouldn't be the last.

Encouraged by Jocelyn's interest, her parents sent her to boarding school in England, where her father had studied. Although she enjoyed French and Latin classes, her favorite subjects were math and physics.

In physics she studied how the universe works—why we don't float away when we jump into the air, how magnets make things stick together, why we can see the moon in daytime. She read about everything from the tiniest atoms to the largest galaxies. By the time she was fifteen, Jocelyn knew she wanted to be an astronomer.

She asked her father to take her to the Armagh Observatory, where he worked as an architect designing a new planetarium. There, she told a staff member of her dream.

"To be a good astronomer," he responded, "you have to be good at staying up late."

Late at night? If there was one thing Jocelyn disliked, it was losing sleep. She enjoyed sleeping much more than staying awake at nighttime!

But Jocelyn was determined not to give up on her dream before she'd even begun. She read about a different kind of telescope, one that could be used in the daytime—a radio telescope. Instead of staring at the stars through a series of lenses and mirrors, Jocelyn would listen to the galaxy, to *hear* what it could tell her.

Jocelyn studied hard at school and college, even when she was the only girl in a class full of boys. While a graduate student at the University of Cambridge, Jocelyn helped to construct a radio telescope. Rather than pointing up to the sky like an optical telescope, this radio telescope was made of wires stretched out across a 4.5-acre field—the size of fifty-seven tennis courts. It had to be large enough to gather information from extremely far away—beyond our solar system. The other students thought Jocelyn would be too "girly" to climb the ladders and twist the wires, but heights didn't scare her.

It took two years,

but in 1967 the radio telescope was ready.

When the telescope was turned on, it took four days to scan the whole sky. Rather than collect light waves, like a typical telescope, large antennas collected radio waves and sent them to a receiver. For months, each sound that the galaxy made was printed out on a giant roll of paper. It was Jocelyn's job to examine every single sound that was drawn on that paper.

Most often, the sound on the paper looked smooth.

⎯⎯⎯⎯⎯⎯⎯

But then in November 1967, she heard something strange. A "scruffy" or "untidy" sound. Little clicks that on paper looked like a mountain range. As regular as a heartbeat.

⎯⌃⎯⌃⎯⌃⎯⌃⎯

But this heart was beating billions of miles away.

"It must be aliens," the professors joked. "Little Green Men
sending signals back to Earth from planets far out in space."
They even named the alien sounds LGM.

But Jocelyn didn't agree. She knew she'd found something *better*. She didn't know what, exactly, but she worked hard, day *and* night, to figure it out, looking through the three miles of paper that the telescope had produced.

It wasn't until Jocelyn found a second set of clicks a week later, from another part of the galaxy, that she grew excited.

It was unlikely that there would be *two* different alien species sending out these sounds—like the ticking of a clock—from space. Every second another tick, tick.

The sounds were coming from a star.

A neutron star.

Stars don't last forever. When they die, stars explode.
What's left behind collapses, shrinking into something small and
very heavy. It spins faster and faster as it shrinks, just like figure
skaters when they tuck their arms in tight. This is a *neutron* star.

As it spins, the star sends radio waves spiraling through the
vacuum of space.

Or at least that's what scientists guessed.
No one had ever found proof.

Until Jocelyn.

Jocelyn discovered that when a neutron star spins, it sends out a beam of radiation, just like a lighthouse's rotating light.

When sailors at sea spot a flashing light, they know there are dangerous rocks ahead.

When Jocelyn heard those pulsing radio waves, timed at just over a second apart, she knew she hadn't discovered Little Green Men. What she *had* discovered was a new type of star—named pulsar for the way it sounds when it spins, like the pulsing beat of a heart.

Detecting pulsars was astounding. Some scientists consider it the greatest astronomical discovery of the twentieth century.

It was an exciting time to be an astronomer.

When newspaper reporters and TV hosts interviewed Jocelyn, however, they often asked more about the new ring on her finger than about her scientific breakthrough.

Jocelyn was proud of both her engagement ring and her achievements. But when she married Martin Burnell a few months later in 1968, many people assumed that she would give up her study of astrophysics. At that time in Britain, it was rare for wives to go to work. Jocelyn wasn't content with that idea though. Why should getting married or having a baby stop her from doing a job that she loved?

$$\rho > \frac{3\pi}{GP^2} = \frac{3\pi}{6.67 \times 10^{-8} \ dyne \ cm^2 \ gm^{-2}}$$

So Jocelyn kept on working.
And discovered more.

Jocelyn Bell Burnell identified the first four neutron stars, ever.

Jocelyn continued to study the mysteries of the universe—becoming a teacher, a researcher, and the head of a university department, as well as serving as president of the Royal Astronomical Society and the Institute of Physics. But in 1974, when the most prestigious award for physics—the Nobel Prize—was awarded for the discovery of pulsars, it went to two male professors who worked with her on the project.

Jocelyn's name was left off the winners' list. She wasn't even mentioned.

Maybe it was because she was a woman. Or because she was young and still a student when she made the discovery. Not being honored for her hard work was unfair, but Jocelyn was gracious. She was excited that the prize had finally been given for an astronomical discovery—for the first time ever.

Jocelyn remained resilient and determined to pursue her dream of learning as much as she could about the stars.

She's won many major awards, from ribbons and medals to being named a dame by the British queen. In 2018 she won the Special Breakthrough Prize in Fundamental Physics and used the $3 million award to set up a fund for young women who want to study the universe.

Jocelyn would go on to work and teach all over the world, helping others discover their own love of physics. Her pioneering research paved the way for new branches of astronomy.

Are there other sounds in the galaxy?
Other types of stars?

Perhaps.

If there are, thanks to Jocelyn, someday they will be heard.

GLOSSARY

astronomer: A person who studies the objects outside of Earth's atmosphere, or the layers of gas that surround the planet.

astrophysics: The use of physics to explain what astronomers find and see. Also includes cosmology, or the study of how the universe started and is changing.

galaxy: A group of millions of stars and planets as well as dust, which moves though the universe. Our solar system is in the Milky Way galaxy.

neutron star: A star that has run out of energy, exploded, and then condensed into a very small, spinning object.

physics: The study of energy and matter and how they are related to each other. It explains gravity and the way things move. It helps us understand energy, such as light, heat, and electricity.

pulsar: A type of neutron star that sends out a beam of radiation when it spins.

radiation: Energy that moves from one place to another in the form of waves or particles. X-rays, light, sound, and heat are all forms of radiation.

radio telescope: A machine, now usually in the shape of a dish, made up of a specialized antenna and a receiver used to collect information about distant objects like stars and black holes.

radio wave: A form of electromagnetic signal that is given off by objects far away in space. Radio waves are similar in shape to ocean waves, with repeating peaks and valleys. Human-made radio waves are used for communication (in televisions, cell phones, GPS, and radios).

receiver: In radio communications, an electronic device that picks up electromagnetic signals, such as radio waves, from space, and turns them into something that people can see, hear, or understand.

solar system: The sun and all the objects that orbit around it, including planets, moons, stars, asteroids, and comets.

universe: Also called the cosmos, this is everything that exists in space and time, including billions of galaxies.